MICHAEL BARRY'S

Salads
THE CRAFTY WAY

JARROLD
PUBLISHING

MICHAEL BARRY'S SALADS THE CRAFTY WAY

Designed and produced by

THE ERSKINE PRESS
Banham, Norwich

for JARROLD PUBLISHING
Whitefriars, Norwich

Recipes by Michael Barry

Food photography by
The Banham Bakehouse, Norfolk

Food styling by Lesley de Boos

Photographs © Andrew Perkins

Designed by Richard Snowball

Text © Michael Barry 1999
This edition © Jarrold Publishing 1999
ISBN 0–7117–1051–1

Printed in Spain

CONTENTS

Introduction

I f, when I say salad, you think 'pickled beetroot', then something is missing and that something is the wonderful, sumptuous range of salads that exists beyond the beetroot scenario. All over the world salads comprise some of the most delicious and fresh-tasting food there is – and you'll find in this book salads from Thailand, the Middle East, Europe, and America, which is perhaps the queen of salad nations. It's only in America that salad has really become a dish in its own right, a main course as often as not, and really quite a substantial one at that.

In many of these salads, lettuce makes no appearance at all, but a whole range of interesting ingredients do, from pasta to asparagus, prawns to mozzarella, rice to aubergines. But that's not to decry lettuce, especially not now that we're blessed with an amazing range of salad leaves available all year round. Lettuces come in three principal categories: first, the buttery, soft, loose-leafed lettuces that are usually good as a background to other more substantial ingredients; second, the Cos lettuces, long, thin-leaved, quite crispy, with a strong and definitive taste. They're delicious on their own and used a lot in America (where they're known as Romaine) to make salads with strong tastes and textures like Caesar salad. They're also used in Middle Eastern salads as spoons, particularly the small, inner leaves that have a curl to them. There's a miniature Cos lettuce widely available in Britain these days called Little Gem, which has the same sort of flavour but only stands about 15 cm/6 in high. Last, but not least, there are the Iceberg or crisp-head lettuces. These are usually the shape of a small football with very crisp leaves, often pale green in colour, tightly wrapped around each other. They're valued for their texture more than for their flavour. I've had them sliced into wedges and served with a thick dressing poured over them, without any further preparation, and very good and filling they were too. They make good bowls for other foods if you peel the leaves off carefully, and shredded they make a wonderful, long-lasting, crisp-textured base for other ingredients.

There is an enormous variety of other basic salad ingredients. Watercress and chicory have been around for quite a while and they're very good additions to any salad; as are the frilly lettuces such as frisée. They often have a slightly heavier texture than other lettuces and a slightly bitter edge, but that's no bad thing because they can be served with more flavoursome or sweeter dressings. There are also Chinese leaves, pale-looking, giant Cos-shaped cabbages that are just as nice eaten raw as they are cooked. And rocket, a peppery green herb, similar in pungency to watercress, which used to be popular in Britain in the seventeenth century and has made a comeback via the popularity of Italian food. Beetroot now comes unpickled and cucumbers come without the ability to repeat as often as they used to.

And while we're on the subject of variety, tomatoes have changed from standard, rather woolly red balls into a wonderful range of flavours, textures and sizes. Starting at the big end, there are the French or Marmande (beefsteak) tomatoes. Real French ones are slightly misshapen, intensely flavoured and make the best tomato salads with a rich vinaigrette dessing and a little chopped onion or chives on top. Cherry tomatoes are my next favourite, at the opposite end of the size scale. Often no more than a mouthful, they're usually very sweet and strongly flavoured. Ordinary tomatoes appear to have been given a push by all this competition because they seem to be grown now for flavour as well as for shape and colour. Plum tomatoes have recently made their appearance, adding another dimension to tomato taste and texture; these are essentially Italian tomatoes used there as much for cooking as for eating in salads. Two other interesting developments are vine-ripened tomatoes and yellow tomatoes, the former usually still on the stalk in the packet. This means that they have been brought to full ripeness on the plant rather than in a ripening room, giving them a greater sweetness and intensity of flavour. There are yellow tomatoes of varying sizes and shapes. Don't be put off by them. Originally, tomatoes in Mexico were fully ripe when green, so yellow ones are a perfectly reasonable variation.

So, all in all, we're extraordinarily well provided with the basics for making salads, though the recipes you'll find in this book offer far more opportunities than that. The French have a great gift for salads with light and crunchy additions such as pine nuts and croutons, while America's substantial salads with chicken and mayonnaise, avocados and fruit are, without question, meals in themselves. The Middle and Far East provide some interesting variations, often with unexpected ingredients like bread or mangoes. These are usually meant to be eaten as part of a meal with two or three other dishes on the table as well, rather than as an accompaniment to a single meat or fish dish. Then there are the really substantial salads meant to be the central starchy part of any meal, based on potatoes, pasta or rice. What unites them all is an interesting combination of contrasts: in texture, crunchy and soft; in taste, fresh and cooked; and in flavour, mild and pungent. Perhaps more than in any other dishes, salads include such a number of these contrasts. Consider, for example, a salad made of quails' eggs with the addition of tomatoes, pine nuts and a vigorous lemon dressing – crisp and soft, sharp and sweet, and a delight to the eye.

All salads need dressing and in this book there are dressings that can be used with all kinds of salads, and those specific to some of the more special salads. Essentially there are the oil and vinegar or lemon-based dressings, often known as French dressing or vinaigrette, and the creamy ones, of which mayonnaise is the best known.

Salad cream, which was the bane of salads of my youth, is an industrial version of a kind of mayonnaise that used to be known as salad sauce and was once made with similar ingredients to mayonnaise. Both vinaigrette and mayonnaise-type dressings are infinitely variable. You can add chopped herbs or other flavourings, you can use different oils, you can add or subtract sugar or cheese, you can whip them, shake them or process them, all providing the most extraordinary variety of flavours and textures. The great thing about most salad dressings is that they can be made in bulk and stored in the fridge. I usually have a couple on the go at any time because they then make putting together a salad really effortless.

A few more thoughts that might be of help all round: first, try and find and keep a good-sized wooden bowl that's just used for salads. After it's been washed and dried for the first time, rub it with a cut clove of garlic, and leave the oils to dry on the wood. Only rinse it from then on without soap. Over the years it will impart a delicate sense of garlic to salads made in the bowl. I've had the same bowl for over thirty-five years and it still gives marvellous and almost daily service. Second, don't dress any green salad more than ten minutes before eating. No lettuce, watercress or other salad leaves will survive the impact of a dressing for long before starting to wilt and lose their texture. (A good trick if you've got slightly wilted lettuce is to rinse it in cold water, shake it dry and put it in a colander in the fridge for ten minutes. It crisps up remarkably well and recovers most of its texture. Always dry lettuce leaves thoroughly before dressing them.) And finally, don't be afraid to eat salad on its own, either as a separate course or, if you fancy a light lunch or supper, as a meal in its own right. Salads, after all, are one of the things that make life really cheerful and summery, whatever the weather or time of year.

Michael Henry

VINAIGRETTES

Known the world over as French dressing, vinaigrettes are very easy to make and are more useful than simply for a green salad. They're probably best made in a food processor or liquidiser because the machine emulsifies the dressing, mixing the oil, vinegar and flavourings thoroughly so they don't separate out easily. It is however quite possible to put the ingredients into a jar with a secure top and just shake thoroughly until the dressing is well mixed. It will separate quite quickly but can always be shaken again. All of these dressings will keep in the fridge for a week or more if in a sealed jar and indeed there is a view that they improve slightly if kept for a day or two.

RED WINE VINAIGRETTE

This is the great southern French-style dressing, wonderful on thick slices of sun-ripened tomatoes, but I find this version nicest with green salads, particularly those made with the slightly bitter lettuces like frisée or curly endive. As with all vinaigrettes the order of mixing is very important as the sugar and salt will not dissolve properly once the oil is added. You can use all olive oil or all sunflower oil if you choose. If using on tomatoes or other solid vegetables, an hour or so marinating in the dressing is a great improvement. If using on greens, dress within 10 minutes of eating.

INGREDIENTS   Makes about 300 ml/10 fl oz

4 tbsp red wine vinegar   **50 ml/2 fl oz olive oil**
½ tsp salt   **175 ml/6 fl oz sunflower oil**
½ tsp sugar

Mix together the vinegar, salt and sugar until the salt and sugar are thoroughly dissolved. Add the olive oil and process or shake again, then add the sunflower oil. Make sure the dressing is thoroughly blended.

WHITE WINE OR CIDER VINEGAR VINAIGRETTE

This is a lighter dressing particularly suitable for white vegetables like cauliflower or potato salad. It also benefits in pungency from the addition of the mustard. If you do not have any grapeseed oil, substitute sunflower oil.

INGREDIENTS   Makes about 300 ml/10 fl oz

4 tbsp white wine or cider vinegar   **½ tsp sugar**
1 tsp Dijon mustard   **50 ml/2 fl oz grapeseed oil**
½ tsp salt   **175 ml/6 fl oz sunflower oil**

Mix the vinegar, mustard, salt and sugar together until the salt and sugar are thoroughly dissolved. Add the grapeseed and sunflower oils and blend or shake until thoroughly mixed.

HERB VINAIGRETTE

This is a particularly nice dressing for salads made of delicate vegetables like French beans or cherry tomatoes or for use on rice or pasta salads. It should be used within 3 or 4 days. The herbs should be finely chopped to make them capable of suspension in the dressing.

INGREDIENTS

Makes about 350 ml/12 fl oz

50 ml/2 fl oz fresh lemon juice
50 ml/2 fl oz white wine or cider vinegar
½ tsp salt
½ tsp sugar

2 tsp each fresh chopped parsley, chives and basil (or use a third of the amount of freeze-dried herbs if fresh are unavailable)
225 ml/8 fl oz sunflower or light vegetable oil

Process or shake the lemon juice, vinegar, salt, sugar and herbs together until the salt and sugar are dissolved. Add the oil and process or shake again.

LEMONETTE DRESSING

This is a dressing from the Middle East where lemon juice is used entirely to replace vinegar as the acidic flavouring in the dressing. It can be used in composite salads like tabbouleh (see page 48), or as a dressing over lentils or other pulses, and very good it is too with a bean salad. I like it best on a Greek salad (see page18); the lemon seems to bring out the flavour of all the other ingredients. Use fresh lemon juice if you can as the flavour really does make a difference.

INGREDIENTS

Makes about 350 ml/12 fl oz

125 ml/4 fl oz fresh lemon juice
½ tsp salt
1 tsp sugar

50 ml/2 fl oz olive oil
175 ml/6 fl oz sunflower or light vegetable oil

Mix the lemon juice, salt and sugar together until the salt and sugar are dissolved. Add the olive oil and process or shake thoroughly. Add the remaining oil and process or shake until the mixture is thoroughly emulsified. This dressing keeps as well as the straight vinaigrettes. If you like you could add some finely chopped fresh herbs.

LIME DRESSING

If you can find them, use the large, green Persian limes for this one.

INGREDIENTS

Makes about 225 ml/8 fl oz

Juice of 2 limes
½ tsp salt
1 tsp soft brown sugar
125 ml/4 fl oz salad oil

Put all the ingredients except the oil into a food processor bowl and process for 3 to 5 seconds; while processing add the oil in a slow steady stream and stop processing as soon as the dressing thickens. This is particularly nice used with shellfish, avocados, flaked white fish and monkfish.

Vinaigrettes and dressings

ITALIAN DRESSING

Create your own Italian-style dressing.

INGREDIENTS
Makes about 150 ml/5 fl oz

2.5 cm/1 in piece spring onion (green part)
1 cm/½ in piece red pepper
1 clove garlic, crushed
½ tsp salt
1 tsp sugar
2 tbsp white wine vinegar or fresh lemon juice
6 tbsp olive or sunflower oil

Finely chop the green spring onion and red pepper. Put these in a jar with the garlic, salt, sugar, vinegar or lemon juice and the oil. Shake or blend really thoroughly and leave to stand for at least an hour before using.

ORIENTAL DRESSING

INGREDIENTS
Makes about 300 ml/10 fl oz

300 ml/10 fl oz white wine vinaigrette (see page 7)
1 tbsp soy sauce
½ clove garlic, crushed
1 tsp crushed fresh ginger (or ½ tsp powdered ginger)

Mix the vinaigrette thoroughly with the soy sauce, garlic and ginger.
Serve straight away.

PESTO DRESSING

This dressing is wonderful with tomatoes.

INGREDIENTS
Makes about 175 ml/6 fl oz

55 g/2 oz pine nuts
25 g/1 oz fresh basil
125 ml/4 fl oz olive oil
1 clove garlic, chopped
40 g/1½ oz freshly grated Parmesan or Pecorino cheese
2 tbsp white wine vinegar
Salt and freshly ground black pepper

Place the pine nuts in a small frying-pan and dry-fry for 3–4 minutes, stirring occasionally until golden. Leave to cool a little, then place them in a food processor or liquidiser with the basil, oil, garlic, cheese, vinegar and seasoning and process until you have a smooth green purée. Store in the refrigerator.

WALNUT OIL DRESSING

You can buy walnut oil from supermarkets or speciality food stores.
You have to remember to put it in the fridge once open, otherwise it goes off.
When fresh, it has a wonderful, rich nutty flavour. This dressing goes well with a
leaf salad containing leaves with a touch of bitterness in them.

INGREDIENTS   Makes about 100 ml/3½ fl oz

Juice of 1 lemon   **½ tsp salt**
1 tsp sugar   **6 tbsp walnut oil**

Put the lemon juice, sugar and salt into a bowl and whisk thoroughly together.
Then add the walnut oil. Whisk until it has emulsified and is smooth and cloudy.

BLUE CHEESE DRESSING

This is an American dressing, made in expensive restaurants by a head waiter
mashing the cheese with a silver fork. It may look good, but no silver fork wielded
by a maître d' ever managed the blend of smoothness and sharpness
achieved by your friendly electric chef.

INGREDIENTS   Makes about 300 ml/10 fl oz

175 g/6 oz blue cheese   **½ tsp sugar**
50 ml/2 fl oz milk   **1 tbsp fresh lemon juice (optional)**
½ tsp made mustard   **150 ml/5 fl oz oil**

Crumble the blue cheese roughly and add it with the milk to a food processor bowl
and blend for about 5 seconds. Scrape down the sides and add mustard, sugar
and the lemon juice if you like your dressings really sharp. Pour in the oil in a slow
steady stream. It should never go in all at once, but be added gradually. As the
oil is added you will notice a change in the noise of the motor and the blades will
slow down suddenly as the dressing becomes thick. The more oil you add,
the thicker it becomes. I like it just this side of softly whipped cream. Try it with
regular salads, or with quarters of washed crisp lettuce such as Iceberg
or Webb's Wonder. Almost a meal in itself.

CRAFTY MAYONNAISE

This recipe produces light, creamy mayonnaise, partly because whole eggs are
used, and partly because blenders or food processors beat in extra air. You can't
make this recipe without a blender or processor, but with one it's effortless.

INGREDIENTS   Makes about 300 ml/10 fl oz

1 egg   **Juice of ½ lemon**
½ tsp salt   **350 ml/12 fl oz olive oil (or olive and/or**
½ tsp sugar   **peanut or sunflower oil)**

Put the egg, salt, sugar and lemon juice into a blender or food processor. Add a
quarter of the oil and blend. Pour the remaining oil into the blender or processor
in a slow steady stream and blend until the mayonnaise is light and creamy.

FARMER'S SALAD

This is the kind of salad that gave French cooking its terrific reputation. While having a bright, sharp flavour, it's also quite substantial, especially if made with one of the crisp heart lettuces such as Iceberg which have such a lot of crunch to them.

INGREDIENTS　　　　　　　　　　　　　　Serves 4

1 Iceberg or other crisp heart lettuce
2 slices white bread
2 tbsp oil
55 g/2 oz crumbly blue cheese (Stilton, Gorgonzola or Roquefort)

FOR THE DRESSING:
2 tbsp wine vinegar
1 tbsp fresh lemon juice
1 tsp sugar
½ tsp salt
6 tbsp salad oil

Wash and dry the lettuce and break into large chunks. Put these in a salad bowl. Cut the bread up into small cubes about 5 mm/¼ in across and fry them till light and gold in the oil then drain them on absorbent paper.

Crumble the cheese with a fork. Shake the dressing ingredients together in a jar. Just before you are ready to serve, sprinkle the cheese over the lettuce, add the cooled croutons and pour over the salad dressing. Toss and turn so that all the lettuce is coated with the dressing and the crunchy bits and cheese are mixed in evenly. Serve in bowls rather than on plates.

CAESAR SALAD

Despite its Roman name, this is an American salad. The mixture of crisp-fried bread cubes, garlic, Parmesan, lettuce and dressing may seem a little unusual at first, but the combination of textures and the freshness and sharpness of the flavours really works. A great family favourite!

INGREDIENTS

1 Cos lettuce
55 g/2 oz croutons
Garlic salt
4 tbsp grated Parmesan cheese

FOR THE DRESSING:　　　　　　Serves 4

1 egg
125 ml/4 fl oz vegetable oil
3 tbsp fresh lemon juice
½ tsp salt
½ tsp sugar

Start by making the dressing: put the egg in boiling water for 1 minute, break into a bowl, add the other dressing ingredients and beat until creamy.
Tear the lettuce into chunks and mix with the croutons in a bowl. Pour the dressing over the salad and mix it all up. Shake a little garlic salt and the Parmesan cheese over the salad and eat immediately!

Farmer's salad with Caesar salad (top)

CHICORY AND ORANGE SALAD

The combination of slightly bitter chicory with the sweetness of oranges makes a marvellous refreshing salad. Add some cottage cheese and you have a delicious, satisfying, low-calorie lunch.

INGREDIENTS

4 medium-sized pieces of chicory
2 large oranges, navel or similar
55 g/2 oz walnuts, crushed (optional)

FOR THE DRESSING:

4 tbsp salad oil (not olive)
2 tbsp fresh lemon juice
½ tsp sugar
½ tsp salt
½ tsp English mustard

Serves 2 as a main course
Serves 4 as a side salad

Rinse and wipe the chicory dry. Trim off the base and slice the chicory across the grain into 5 mm/¼ in rounds. Put these into a bowl, breaking them up slightly with your fingers to separate the rings.

Peel the oranges, removing as much of the white pith as possible. Slice them in half, then slice them across the grain into 5 mm/¼ in slices as well. Remove any pips. Add the oranges to the chicory and mix gently together.

Put the salad oil, lemon juice, sugar, salt and mustard into a screw-top jar and shake well, or whisk all the dressing ingredients together in a bowl. Pour over the salad, toss it well and allow it to stand for the flavours to develop for 15 minutes before serving. If you are using the crushed walnuts, sprinkle them generously over the salad. They add a lovely crunch.

Chicory and orange salad

SIMPLE SPINACH SALAD

A salad made of small, crisp fresh spinach leaves of a deep, rich green is one of my great delights. Buy ready-prepared baby spinach leaves if you can get them. You just need to rinse them through before using them. This is the perfect salad for lunch, served on its own with just some warm crusty French bread, and it's also good served after a main course.

INGREDIENTS
Serves 4

450 g/1 lb young spinach leaves
Salt and freshly ground black pepper
1 tbsp runny honey
1 tbsp fresh lemon juice
2 tbsp oil – sunflower or safflower

FOR THE CROUTONS:
2 slices wholemeal bread
1–2 tbsp oil
1 tsp dried mixed herbs

To make the croutons, cut the bread into small cubes of about 1 cm/½ in and fry them in a little oil until pale gold. Drain well on kitchen paper and sprinkle with the herbs.

Wash and dry the spinach well if you haven't bought it ready prepared, and tear the leaves into pieces. Don't cut the leaves as they'll go floppy.
Season generously with salt and pepper.

Gently heat the honey and lemon juice together in a saucepan until the honey melts. Then add the oil, stir, and when the dressing is hot, pour it over the spinach and serve at once with the croutons sprinkled over the top.

GREEN SALAD
WITH LEMONETTE DRESSING

Choose any of the enormous range of salad leaves available these days: Oak Leaf, Iceberg and mini-Cos lettuces in the summer; radicchio and frilly lettuces in the autumn; Chinese leaves, chicory and endive in the winter and spring. Aim to vary flavour and texture as well as colour.

INGREDIENTS
Mixed salad leaves
1 quantity Lemonette dressing (see page 8)

Wash the leaves, tear them into small pieces and put them in a salad bowl. Dress the salad with the lemonette dressing just before you serve it, and toss it thoroughly so that the leaves are all well coated.

Simple spinach salad and Green salad with lemonette dressing (top)

GREEK SALAD

There are wonderful varieties of tomatoes in the shops, and for this salad you need large ones with a good full flavour. Most supermarkets now stock feta cheese – it's white and crumbly with a lovely tang.

INGREDIENTS   Serves 4

450 g/1 lb beefsteak or plum tomatoes
½ Spanish onion, peeled
55 g/2 oz feta cheese
½ tsp freeze-dried thyme
½ tsp freeze-dried oregano

FOR THE DRESSING:

6 tbsp olive oil
3 tbsp fresh lemon juice
Pinch salt
Pinch sugar

Slice the tomatoes into 5 mm/¼ in rounds and arrange on a shallow dish. Slice the onion as finely as possible and sprinkle over the tomatoes. Crumble the feta cheese over the top of that, then sprinkle on the herbs.

In a bowl mix together the dressing ingredients – olive oil, lemon juice, salt and sugar and pour over the salad. Let the flavours develop for at least half an hour in the fridge. This will keep happily for up to 3 hours before serving.

TOMATO SALAD
WITH PESTO DRESSING

This salad is dressed with pesto sauce, a speciality of that bit of the Mediterranean that runs from Nice in France down to Genoa in Italy. It's made with slight variations along the coast. All versions, however, share a particular affinity to tomatoes, as does the basic herb, basil.

INGREDIENTS   Serves 4 as a starter

450 g/1 lb tomatoes, large or small, but ripe!
1 quantity Pesto dressing (see page 10)
Basil leaves, to garnish
Crusty bread, to serve

Slice the tomatoes, if large, into 5 mm/¼ in thick slices and lay them in an attractive pattern in a shallow china dish. If using cherry tomatoes, halve these and place in the same sort of container. Drizzle the pesto dressing over the tomatoes and leave to marinate for at least half an hour – up to 2 or 3 hours in the fridge is fine. Garnish with a few basil leaves and serve with crusty bread.

Greek salad (top) and Tomato salad with pesto dressing

A SALAD OF SCALLOPS AND ASPARAGUS

This is an unashamedly luxurious dish but one with a combination of such intense flavours that a little goes a long way. Scallops are one of the most delicate and most readily acceptable of shellfish – gleaming white and quite chewily textured. The classic ways to serve them are in thick and often cheesy sauces but this salad, with the fish served warm, is a revelation of texture and flavour.

INGREDIENTS
Serves 4

4 large scallops, shelled
225 g/8 oz asparagus
55 g/2 oz pine nuts
2 tbsp olive oil
1 frilly Lollo Rosso-type lettuce
Salt and freshly ground black pepper

FOR THE DRESSING:
6 tbsp salad oil
1 tsp sugar
1 tsp salt
1 tbsp red wine vinegar
1 tbsp fresh lemon juice

Remove the coral half-moons from the scallops and set them aside. Cut the main body of each scallop across the grain into 3 slices. Trim the asparagus, getting rid of any hard bits of stalk, and steam in a colander over boiling water for 9 minutes.

Fry the pine nuts in olive oil for 2 minutes until golden brown, making sure they don't burn. Remove the nuts and reserve the oil in the pan. Wash and drain the lettuce and tear it into pieces about half the size of a postcard. Fill 4 elegant bowls with lettuce. Let the asparagus cool a little and lay it on the lettuce then sprinkle the top of each with pine nuts.

Mix the dressing ingredients together in a screw-top jar and shake vigorously. Reheat the oil you cooked the pine nuts in until it's very hot and add the slices of scallop. Cook for 1 minute on each side, add the coral half-moons, season with a little salt and pepper, and cook 1 minute more. Place the scallops on the lettuce, asparagus and pine nuts, pour 2 tablespoons of dressing over each bowl and serve whilst still warm.

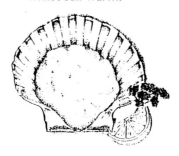

A salad of scallops and asparagus

CRAFTY PEPERONATA

This is an Italian-style salad which, in its original form, required a lot of complex grilling and peeling of the peppers. This is to get rid of the rather waxy outside coating but the crafty method here allows that same coating to be cooked off without too much fiddling about.

INGREDIENTS   Serves 4

700 g/1 lb 9 oz mixed sweet peppers (orange, yellow and red)
2 tbsp olive oil
1 clove garlic
Juice of 1 lemon
Salt and freshly ground black pepper
1 tbsp chopped parsley

Halve the peppers and remove the seeds. Slice across into 5 mm/¼ in strips. Heat the oil in a frying-pan that will take all the peppers. Peel and finely chop the garlic and add this to the oil. Immediately add the pepper slices and turn them over a medium to high heat for 2 to 3 minutes. Season and turn the heat down and allow the peppers to cook gently for about 10 minutes until they are just beginning to caramelise.

Squeeze the lemon juice over the peppers, turn thoroughly and allow to cool. Season to taste and sprinkle with parsley before serving with crusty bread or as part of a buffet.

MORS' CUCUMBER SALAD

This is a simple method for making cucumber salad that comes from Denmark. It's quite delicious and goes perfectly with hot or cold salmon.

INGREDIENTS

1 large cucumber
125 ml/4 fl oz cider vinegar
125 ml/4 fl oz boiled water, allowed to cool
55 g/2 oz sugar
1 tsp salt

Wash and trim the cucumber and slice as thinly as possible; a food processor or mandolin is ideal for this job. Put the slices into a china or glass bowl.

In a separate bowl, mix the vinegar, water, sugar and salt and stir until the sugar and salt are dissolved. Pour over the cucumber and allow to marinate for at least 2 hours and up to 12 hours before serving.

Crafty peperonata

WILD MUSHROOM SALAD

Although the recipe states wild mushrooms, it's now possible to make this salad with some of the new varieties of cultivated mushrooms available on the market, especially oyster or champignon mushrooms, which are a halfway-house between the real wild ones and old-fashioned domesticated ones. The salad is a smashing accompaniment to simply grilled meat but also suitable as a course on its own.

INGREDIENTS
Serves 4

450 g/1 lb wild mushrooms,
  washed but not peeled
1 clove garlic, chopped
2 tbsp olive oil
2 tbsp fresh lemon juice

½ tsp caster sugar
Salt and freshly ground black pepper
Lettuce, radishes and sorrel leaves
  (for the salad base), shredded
2 tsps chopped parsley and chives

Slice the mushrooms and sauté them with the garlic in 1 tablespoon of hot oil for 2 minutes. Do not let them burn. Mix the lemon juice with the sugar until this has dissolved. Place the garlic mushrooms in a bowl and, while still warm, toss with the remaining oil and the lemon juice mixture. Season, then cool.

To serve, make beds of shredded salad. Sprinkle with chopped herbs, and pour on the mushrooms and dressing.

AVOCADO, TOMATO AND MOZZARELLA SALAD

This salad represents the Italian flag and is always dressed with the bright green leaves of fresh basil. If you're going to keep it at all, squeeze a little lemon juice over the avocado, cover with cling film and put it in the fridge. The real *mozzarella di bufola* or buffalo milk mozzarella from Naples has a unique texture and flavour.

INGREDIENTS
Serves 4 as a starter

2 small ripe avocados
4 ripe tomatoes, thinly sliced
115 g/4 oz mozzarella, thinly sliced

FOR THE DRESSING:
2 tbsp red wine vinegar
½ tsp sugar
6 tbsp olive oil
Salt and freshly ground black pepper
2 tbsp shredded fresh basil

Cut the avocados in half and remove the stone. Peel the skin off carefully in long ribbons. Place each half cut face down onto a chopping-board and slice it almost through lengthways, leaving a hinge on the thin end. Put each sliced half onto a plate and press down a little and you'll find it will fan out into an attractive shape. Arrange the tomato slices with alternate slices of mozzarella.

Place the vinegar, sugar, oil and plenty of seasoning into a screw-topped jar and shake until well combined. Drizzle over the salads and scatter the basil on top.

Wild mushroom salad (top) with Avocado, tomato and mozzarella salad

THREE-BEAN SALAD

This is a salad made from beans, some fresh and some canned, which go together deliciously in terms of texture and taste. The crafty way to make this is to use canned beans for two of the ingredients, although you could if you wished start with dried ones, soaking them for 6 hours and then boiling them for 2 hours before using them. The great trick with canned beans and other legumes is to refresh them in cold running water before using them.

INGREDIENTS   Serves 4–6

225 g/8 oz fresh French beans
425 g/15 oz can cannellini beans
425 g/15 oz can red kidney beans
1 small red or mild white onion
1 tbsp chopped fresh parsley

FOR THE DRESSING:

4 tbsp olive or sunflower oil
2 tbsp fresh lemon juice
2 tsp Dijon mustard
½ tsp salt
1 tsp caster sugar

Trim the French beans, cut in half and cook them for 4–5 minutes in a pan of boiling salted water. Drain and plunge into cold water to stop any further cooking. Put the canned beans into a sieve. Wash them thoroughly under running cold water and then leave them to stand in a basin of cold water for 5 minutes. Rinse again and drain well.

Peel and halve the onion and slice it very finely. Whisk together the oil, lemon juice, mustard, salt and sugar. Mix all the beans together in a large bowl and add the onion slices and then the dressing. Stir gently and sprinkle with chopped parsley.

Three-bean salad

CHINESE LEAF
AND RED PEPPER SALAD

This salad combines the crisp ingredients often found in a Chinese stir-fry vegetable dish but eaten as a salad without cooking. The delicious peanut dressing is one that's often used in South East Asia to eat with vegetables or vegetable salads, and although the ingredients may seem unusual, it's worth trying – you'll be converted without very much effort. It makes a good first course for a substantial meal or can be eaten with one or two other Chinese-style dishes as part of an Eastern dinner in its own right.

INGREDIENTS
Serves 4

450 g/1 lb Chinese leaves, finely shredded
1 red pepper
115 g/4 oz bamboo shoots (canned), drained
225 g/8 oz beansprouts
115 g/4 oz carrots, peeled and cut into matchsticks
Coriander leaves, to garnish

FOR THE DRESSING:
55 g/2 oz roasted peanuts
125 ml/4 fl oz soy sauce
50 ml/2 fl oz cider or rice wine vinegar
2 tsp caster sugar
125 ml/4 fl oz water
Small bunch fresh coriander (parsley will do as an alternative)

Cut the Chinese leaves in half lengthwise and then slice across into 1 cm/½ in ribbons, discarding the heavy core at the base. Slice the red pepper into fine strips. Cut the bamboo shoots into 1 cm/½ in slices and then across again into matchstick-shaped shreds. Mix the Chinese leaves, pepper, shredded bamboo shoots, beansprouts and carrots together in a large bowl.

Put the dressing ingredients into a blender or food processor and process until well blended. Pour over the salad ingredients, toss thoroughly, garnish with coriander leaves and serve within half an hour of dressing.

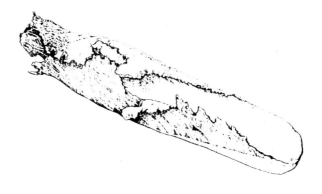

Chinese leaf and red pepper salad

TUNISIAN CARROT SALAD

This is a bright, vivid salad both in appearance and flavour and makes a tasty though not too substantial starter for a meal with other exotic flavours in it. As with so many similar dishes, there are variations and versions for almost every household in North Africa, but this crafty version incorporates our liking for vegetables that still have a little crispness and bite to them.

INGREDIENTS   Serves 4

700g/1 lb 9 oz carrots
2 cloves garlic
125 ml/4 fl oz olive oil
½ tsp ground turmeric
½ tsp ground cumin
1 tsp caster sugar
½ tsp salt
Juice and grated rind of 1 lemon
Mixed salad leaves, to serve

Peel the carrots and cut them into 5–7.5 cm/2–3 in lengths and then split these lengths into batons approximately 5 mm/¼ in across.

Peel and chop the garlic and add that to the olive oil in a heavy saucepan. Add the spices and cook gently until the garlic is pale gold but not burned. Add the carrot batons and turn them thoroughly in the spice mixture and cook over a very gentle heat for 5 minutes. Barely cover the carrots with water, add the sugar and salt, and bring to the boil. Simmer for 7–8 minutes, checking to make sure you don't overcook the carrots. They should still retain a little crispness.

Allow the carrots to cool in their liquid then drain them and put them in a dish. Sprinkle with the lemon rind and pour over the lemon juice, turning them thoroughly. Chill for an hour before eating. Serve on some mixed salad leaves.

Tunisian carrot salad

AUBERGINE SALAD

There are many different ways of making aubergines into a cold dish, some are very complex and some are very simple. This is rather a simple version which benefits from being one of the rare ones that doesn't include tomato.

INGREDIENTS

Serves 4

900 g/2 lb aubergines, preferably large ones
150 ml/5 fl oz olive oil

FOR THE DRESSING:

3 tbsp red wine vinegar
½ tsp salt
1 tsp sugar
1 tsp fresh oregano, or ½ tsp freeze-dried
Pinch of thyme

There was a time when aubergines needed salting before cooking in order to draw out the bitter juices, but most aubergines these days are bred not to have this problem. You can, however, if you like, salt the aubergine slices for half an hour before proceeding, remembering to rinse off the salt before frying.

Take the caps off the aubergines and slice them lengthways into 1 cm/½ in slices. Salt or not, as you choose (see above), and then fry them in a large pan in the olive oil until they're light golden brown on both sides. You may need to add a little extra olive oil as nothing absorbs oil quite as much as aubergines. When they're cooked, place them on an oval platter, overlapping only a little.

Mix the vinegar, salt, sugar and herbs together and, using a spoon, sprinkle the dressing over the aubergines. Turn a couple of times to make sure that the mixture coats both sides and leave to marinate for at least 30 minutes and up to 2 hours before serving.

Aubergine salad

MIDDLE EASTERN BREAD SALAD

In the Middle East they have a rather more generous view of what makes a good salad than we tend to in Europe. Bread, after all, is not the first thing that springs to mind. But this is not only a delicious recipe, it's also extremely economical. Until you've tasted the salad though, you must not try to adjust the seasonings to Western tastes. It may seem too lemony, but when you taste it you will find the balance actually does work, and very well. A word of warning though: you really do need a food processor to make this effortlessly.

INGREDIENTS   Serves 4

1 good-sized bunch parsley
4 tbsp salad oil
6 tbsp fresh lemon juice
2 tsp sugar
1 tsp salt
8 radishes
225 g/8 oz tomatoes
1 bunch spring onions
6 thick slices white bread
Heart of a Cos lettuce

Put the parsley into the processor bowl and process until finely chopped. Add the oil, lemon juice, sugar, salt, washed and trimmed radishes, quartered tomatoes, and trimmed spring onions. Process until thoroughly blended and the vegetables are chopped into fairly small flakes, then transfer the mixture into another bowl.

Without washing the processor bowl or blade, put in the slices of bread, broken into rough chunks, and process until you have fine breadcrumbs (you may have to scrape the bowl down a couple of times). Add 125 ml/4 fl oz water and process again for 3 seconds to mix thoroughly. Take out and mix the breadcrumbs with the vegetable dressing. Taste for seasoning. It may need a little more liquid, in which case add up to another 225 ml/8 fl oz water to moisten the breadcrumbs.

Line a dish with the inner leaves of the Cos lettuce and fill the centre with the bread salad.

Middle Eastern bread salad

QUAILS' EGG SALAD WITH TOMATOES AND PINE NUTS

My memories of the Lebanon include some of the most exotic food I've ever eaten, and one of these was a set of hors-d'œuvres eaten in an extremely grand gathering where the servants were so refined they never spoke, even when spoken to. It was the first time I had ever eaten quails' eggs; tiny, intense mouthfuls that are much favoured in the Middle East. They're widely available in the UK, both fresh and smoked and even pickled, so you can try this salad without any difficulty.

INGREDIENTS

24 quails' eggs
24 cherry tomatoes
55 g/2 oz pine nuts
1 tbsp olive oil
Dark green lettuce leaves, to serve (optional)

FOR THE DRESSING:

100 ml/3½ fl oz olive oil
2 tbsp red wine vinegar
½ tsp salt
½ tsp sugar

Serves 4

Boil the quails' eggs gently for about 6 minutes. Cool and shell carefully.
Cut the cherry tomatoes in half. Fry the pine nuts in a tablespoon of olive oil
until golden brown – do not let them burn!

Lay the quails' eggs and tomatoes in an attractive pattern either in a pretty dish
or on a bed of large dark green lettuce leaves. Sprinkle the pine nuts over the top.
Shake the olive oil, vinegar, salt and sugar together in a jar until thoroughly
mixed. Pour over the salad and serve after 10 minutes. The dish can be kept
a little longer but doesn't improve after half an hour.

RAITA (YOGHURT) SALAD

Wonderfully cooling with all spicy dishes, this is a classic of North Indian cookery.

INGREDIENTS

2 ripe tomatoes
10 cm/4 in chunk cucumber, quartered lengthways
3 spring onions, trimmed

FOR THE DRESSING:

1 tbsp fresh lemon juice
150 ml/¼ pint natural yoghurt
1 tsp salt
1 tsp freeze-dried mint
1 tsp freeze-dried parsley

Chop the tomatoes into pea-sized pieces in a bowl to save the juice.
Do the same with the cucumber and spring onions and add to the tomatoes.
Stir the lemon juice into the yoghurt with the salt and herbs and mix with the
vegetables. If possible, leave to mature for an hour before eating.

Quails' egg salad with tomatoes and pine nuts

POTATO AND WATERCRESS SALAD

A nice contrast between creamy potatoes and
peppery watercress makes this a delicious salad.

INGREDIENTS
Serves 6–8

900 g/2 lb salad potatoes (Fir Apple, Kipfler or other new potatoes)
Juice of 1 lemon
½ tsp sea salt
2 large bunches watercress
6 tbsp mayonnaise
1 tsp made mustard

Peel or scrape the potatoes, cut them into evenly-sized pieces and boil in salted
water until just tender. Drain and put them in a bowl, pour over the lemon juice,
add the sea salt and allow them to cool.

Wash the watercress if necessary, cut off the stalks and cut these into 5 mm/¼ in
pieces. Gently mix them with the potatoes, the mayonnaise and the mustard. Chop
the watercress leaves very roughly and place over the top of the salad as a garnish.
This salad can be made up to 24 hours in advance if kept covered in the fridge.

NEW POTATO SALAD WITH DILL

A lovely, creamy potato salad, especially good with fish.

INGREDIENTS
Serves 6–8

1.3 kg/3 lb small new potatoes
3 tbsp chopped fresh dill
85 g/3 oz mayonnaise
55 g/2 oz natural yoghurt
1 tsp fresh lemon juice
1 tsp Dijon mustard
1 tbsp clear honey
Salt and freshly ground black pepper
Tiny dill sprigs, to garnish

Place the potatoes in a large pan of boiling salted water and cook for
15–20 minutes until tender. Drain and leave to cool a little.

Meanwhile, mix together the dill, mayonnaise, yoghurt, lemon juice, mustard
and honey in a large serving-bowl. Season well. Stir the drained potatoes into
the dill sauce while they're still warm, then chill thoroughly.
Garnish with dill sprigs just before serving.

Potato and watercress salad (top) and New potato salad with dill

HOT POTATO SALAD

Here's an alternative way of serving a potato salad, in this case hot. It's an
American tradition, usually eaten with things like salt beef sandwiches, but it's a
great favourite in our house, especially with young people.

INGREDIENTS   Serves 4

450 g/ 1 lb freshly boiled potatoes
1 tbsp cider vinegar
½ tsp salt
4 tbsp mayonnaise
1 bunch spring onions, finely chopped

Roughly chop the hot boiled potatoes and sprinkle with the cider vinegar and salt.
Stir in the mayonnaise and chopped spring onions. Serve at once.

SIMPLE PASTA SALAD

Make a lot of this salad as in my experience people come back for second,
if not third, helpings. It's also cheap and very quick to make. It's best made
with short, fat pasta – penne, spirals, shells, but nothing long and
straggly like spaghetti or tagliatelle.

INGREDIENTS   Serves 4

225 g/8 oz pasta
1 bulb fennel
175–225 g/6–8 oz 'exotic' frozen mixed vegetables (with peppers, sweetcorn, etc.)
4 tbsp mayonnaise – either home-made or a good bought one
Juice and grated rind of 1 lemon, preferably unwaxed
Salt and freshly ground black pepper

Cook the pasta until *al dente,* drain it in a colander (do not throw away all the
hot water) then pour a jug of cold water over it to stop it sticking.
Make sure the pasta is thoroughly drained.

Chop the fennel bulb into pea-sized pieces. Boil the frozen vegetables in some of
the reserved pasta water for no more than thirty seconds; just long enough
to defrost them. Drain the vegetables and pour cold water over them to
stop them cooking further.

In a big bowl, stir the pasta with all the vegetables until they're thoroughly mixed.
Stir the mayonnaise, the juice and grated rind of the lemon and the seasoning
together and dress the pasta salad, garnishing with fennel.
Leave it to develop the flavours for about half an hour before serving.
It's a wonderful combination of richness, colour, crunch and sharpness.

Simple pasta salad

FARFALLE SALMON SALAD

A light, summery pasta salad with a lemon and herb dressing
to bring out the flavour of the salmon.

INGREDIENTS

Serves 4

1 salmon steak, about 115 g/4 oz in weight
115 g/8 oz farfalle pasta (bows)
115 g/4 oz sugar snap peas

FOR THE DRESSING:

4 tbsp olive oil
1 tbsp white wine vinegar
1 tsp sugar
Juice and grated rind of ½ lemon
2 tbsp chopped fresh herbs, such as parsley, chervil, fennel or dill
Salt and freshly ground black pepper

Place the salmon in a large pan of boiling salted water and simmer gently for
5 minutes. Check if it's cooked by inserting a fork to see if the bone comes
away from the flesh. Remove with a slotted spoon (reserving the water),
drain well and divide into large flakes, discarding the bones and skin.

Return the water to the boil, tip in the pasta and cook for 10–12 minutes until
al dente. Drain, then rinse quickly under cold running water. Meanwhile,
cut the sugar snap peas in half and place in a pan of lightly salted boiling water.
Boil for 1 minute, drain and rinse under cold running water.

To make the dressing, whisk together the olive oil, wine vinegar, sugar
and lemon juice. Stir in the grated lemon rind and half the chopped herbs.
Season to taste. Toss the pasta in the dressing while it's still warm.
Add the salmon flakes, sugar snap peas and remaining herbs and
toss gently to combine. Serve cool or cold.

Farfalle salmon salad

WILD RICE SALAD

This dish is rather like a vegetarian kedgeree that has the freshness and luxury of asparagus to give it an extra lift. The combination of wild and traditional rice gives the whole dish an excitement both in appearance and flavour.

INGREDIENTS

Serves 6

225 g/8 oz American easy-cook long grain and wild rice mixture
Pinch of salt
450 g/1 lb fresh asparagus
1 bunch spring onions (about 6)
55 g/2 oz pecan or walnut halves

FOR THE DRESSING:

2 tbsp fresh lemon juice
1 tbsp clear honey
1 tsp chilli sauce
4 tbsp sunflower oil

Cook the rice according to the instructions on the packet (usually twice the amount of liquid to rice and about 15–18 minutes cooking-time with a pinch of salt). Drain and allow to cool slightly in a sealed bowl.

Trim and clean the asparagus, cutting off any woody bits, then cut the asparagus spears into 2.5 cm/1 in lengths. Trim the spring onions and cut into 1 cm/½ in lengths. Split the pecan or walnut halves in half lengthways.
Mix together the dressing ingredients, starting with the lemon juice and honey and adding the chilli sauce and oil afterwards, whisking to combine.

Bring a small pan of water to the boil, add the asparagus pieces and cook for just 2–3 minutes. Add the spring onions, remove from the boil and drain immediately, reserving a couple of tablespoons of the cooking-water. Add this water to the dressing. Mix the hot vegetables into the warm rice, saving a few pieces of asparagus for the garnish. Add the nuts and the dressing and stir and toss thoroughly. Serve warm, although it's perfectly edible cold.

Wild rice salad

ALMOND AND AVOCADO RICE SALAD

This combines the crunch of almonds, the nutty textures and flavours of brown rice and the soft melting qualities of avocado. It's very easy to buy easy-cook brown rice these days which makes life much quicker as it takes only half the time to cook as the old-fashioned kind. Lay the salad out on an oval serving-dish and decorate as prettily as you can.

INGREDIENTS

175 g/6 oz easy-cook brown rice
Pinch of salt
1 tsp salad oil
4 spring onions
6 cherry tomatoes
55 g/2 oz almonds, cut into slivers

1 tbsp chopped parsley
1 large, ripe avocado

FOR THE DRESSING:

4 tbsp salad or olive oil
2 tbsp fresh lemon or lime juice
½ tsp salt
1 tsp sugar

Serves 4

Measure the rice into a cup and put it into a saucepan. Measure twice the volume of water as you had of rice in the same cup, pour it in, adding a pinch of salt and a teaspoon of salad oil. Bring to the boil, cover, turn the heat right down to low and simmer for 20–25 minutes.

Meanwhile, clean and finely chop the spring onions and wash and halve the tomatoes. Toast the almonds in a dry frying-pan or under the grill for a couple of minutes until they're pale gold.

Mix all the dressing ingredients together – oil, juice, salt and sugar – and either whisk or shake in a sealed jar. When the rice is cooked, put it into a sieve and run cold water through it for a minute until it has cooled. Drain thoroughly and place in a bowl. Add the chopped spring onions, half the chopped parsley and half the salad dressing and stir till mixed. Put a layer on the serving-dish or plate you're going to use, arrange the tomatoes, cut side up, decoratively around it and sprinkle over the toasted almonds.

Halve the avocado, remove the stone, cut each half into quarters and peel the skin off very carefully. Put each avocado quarter, sharp end away from you, onto a chopping-board and, with a sharp knife, cut it lengthways into four or five slivers without cutting through the tip. Press down gently with the heel of your hand and you'll have a fan of avocado. Repeat with the remaining quarters and place attractively on the rice salad. Pour the remaining dressing over the avocados and sprinkle with chopped parsley. Covered lightly with clingfilm, this can be chilled in the fridge for up to 6–8 hours before serving.

Almond and avocado rice salad

TABBOULEH
(CRACKED WHEAT SALAD)

This is a very nutritious and delicious salad which is becoming increasingly fashionable in restaurants. Its basic ingredient is cracked wheat, widely available and sold under the name of bulgar wheat, bourghul or podghuri, depending on its source of origin.

INGREDIENTS   Serves 4

175 g/6 oz bulgar wheat
1 bunch spring onions (about 6)
225 g/8 oz plum tomatoes
½ cucumber
Couple of mint sprigs
55 g/2 oz chopped fresh parsley
3 tbsp olive oil
Juice of 1 lemon
200 g/7 oz feta cheese
Salt and freshly ground black pepper
1 small Cos lettuce
Hot pitta or French bread, to serve

Put the bulgar wheat in a bowl and cover with boiling water.
It will absorb much of the water and swell up within 30 minutes.

Meanwhile, clean and trim the spring onions, wash the tomatoes, halve the cucumber lengthways and remove the seeds. Reserving 2 or 3 tomatoes, roughly chop all the vegetables – you could do this in a food processor – along with the mint and parsley.

When the bulgar wheat has absorbed most of the water, drain it well and stir in the olive oil and lemon juice and then the chopped vegetables and feta cheese, seasoning it generously with salt and pepper. The bulgar wheat will absorb some of the flavours and juices of the vegetables.

Line a bowl with the washed and separated leaves of the Cos lettuce and spoon the wheat mixture into the middle. Roughly chop the remaining tomatoes and arrange them in the middle of the tabbouleh. Each person serves themselves by taking a couple of lettuce leaves and some spoonfuls of the mixture, with slices of hot pitta or French bread. Traditionally, the Cos lettuce leaves are used as a 'spoon'.

Tabbouleh

SALADE NIÇOISE

This is the classic Mediterranean salad, originally from the countryside around Nice and perfect for lunch on a hot day. Use the best ingredients, crisp green lettuce, sweet tomatoes, Jersey Royal potatoes, and serve in the prettiest salad bowl you have!

INGREDIENTS

Serves 4

225 g/8 oz new potatoes – Jersey Royals if you can get them
225 g/8 oz stringless green beans – the really thin ones
1 Webb's Wonder or Cos lettuce
225 g/8 oz tomatoes – preferably tiny cherry ones
4 hard-boiled eggs
185 g/6½ oz tin tuna fish
6–8 anchovy fillets
Black olives, optional
Crusty bread, to serve

FOR THE DRESSING:

4 tbsp olive oil
2 tbsp fresh lemon juice
Pinch of salt
Pinch of sugar

Boil the potatoes until they're just tender and the trimmed stringless beans until they're still slightly crunchy. Plunge the beans into cold water to cool. Wash and dry the lettuce and tear it into quite small pieces. Put it into a large bowl – perhaps one of those lovely white china ones – this salad looks so pretty that it's worth making in a super container. Spread the lettuce out in the bowl.

Wash the tomatoes, halve them if they're cherry ones, or cut them into quarters if they're bigger, and put them in a ring just inside the edge of the lettuce. Shell the hard-boiled eggs and cut them into quarters and put them in a ring so that you have a ring of green, a ring of red, and a ring of white and yellow. Then put the beans in a ring followed by a ring of potatoes. You may have to cut these in half unless they're really small. You now have a series of wonderful concentric circles. Into the middle of that you pile the slightly broken-up tuna fish. If it's in brine, drain it first; if in oil, then you can put it straight onto the salad, pouring the oil over the top. Separate the anchovy fillets and arrange them with the olives in a decorative pattern over the salad – a lattice design looks very effective.

Mix the four ingredients for the dressing together and give it a good whisk until it's thick. Pour it over the salad and serve immediately with hot crusty French bread. Don't toss this salad, you'll spoil the look of it!

Salade niçoise

CALIFORNIA LAYERED SALAD

Not surprisingly, California salad is an American-style dish meant to be eaten as a
first or a main course, including sweet as well as savoury components.
It's a mixture of fruit, salad vegetables and low-fat cottage cheese.
As with a lot of these kinds of salad, the physical layout is all-important so
that the mixture and combinations look attractive as well as tasting good.
You can layer this up in a large glass bowl ready to serve or just use any plastic
bowl that is the correct size and turn it out for a spectacular effect.

INGREDIENTS　　　　　Serves 8–10

1 medium-sized melon
1 large mango
1 red pepper
2 Little Gem lettuces, washed
225 g/8 oz strawberries
225 g/8 oz low-fat cottage cheese with pineapple
175 g/6 oz beansprouts

FOR THE DRESSING:

4 tbsp sunflower oil
2 tbsp fresh lemon juice
½ tsp salt
½ tsp sugar
1 tsp wholegrain mustard

Divide the melon into four and remove the seeds. Cut each quarter away from the
peel and chop into 1 cm/½ in pieces. Slice the cheeks off the mango, halve each
cheek, remove the peel and cut into 1 cm/½ in pieces. Take the top off the red
pepper, remove the seeds and cut into thin rings. Slice the lettuces across the grain
into 5 mm/¼ in ribbons. Hull the strawberries and cut into slices.

Put the oil, lemon juice, salt, sugar and mustard in a screw-topped jar and shake
together until well mixed. Place the red pepper rings in the bottom of a
3.5-litre/6-pint bowl and put the melon pieces on top. Spoon over the cottage
cheese and arrange the sliced strawberries on top. Next put in the mango pieces
and the beansprouts and finish with the shredded lettuce. Drizzle over the
dressing; you can chill this salad for up to half an hour before serving.

To serve, turn out onto a plate to show off the colourful layers.

California layered salad

WARM DUCK SALAD

A salad which makes one duck go a long way – and you'll still have the legs left to grill for another light meal. You will need to marinade the duck, ideally the night before.

INGREDIENTS

1 x 1.8 kg/4 lb duckling, or 4 duck breast portions (skinned)
2 tbsp olive oil
Fried bread croutons, to serve

FOR THE MARINADE:

2 tbsp soy sauce
1 tbsp dry sherry
1 tbsp olive oil
1 tbsp fresh orange juice
1 tsp salt
1 tsp ground coriander
1 tsp ground ginger
1 tsp ground mace or nutmeg
1 clove garlic, crushed

FOR THE DRESSING:

150 ml/5 fl oz olive oil
75 ml/2½ fl oz fresh orange juice
1 tbsp red wine vinegar
1 tsp honey
Salt and freshly ground black pepper
1 tsp mild French mustard
1 tsp finely grated orange rind

Serves 4

FOR EACH SERVING OF SALAD:

2 good curly endive leaves
2 radicchio leaves
1 slice beefsteak tomato
2–3 slices cucumber
1 artichoke bottom or 1 tinned artichoke heart
1 black olive, pitted

Have your butcher remove and skin the duck breasts and cut off the legs; keep them to use on another occasion, and keep the carcass to use for stock.
Make 5 or 6 small incisions into the fleshy side of the breasts, about 5 mm/¼ in deep, running right across. Arrange, cut sides up, in a shallow dish.
Mix all the ingredients for the marinade together and pour over the duck breasts. Now turn the breasts cut sides down and leave for 12 hours, or overnight.

To make the salad, heat 2 tablespoons of olive oil in a frying-pan until smoking. Remove the breasts from the marinade, place in the pan and seal on both sides. Lower the heat a little and fry the breasts for 3 minutes on each side if you like the meat to be pink, a little longer for well done. Remove the breasts to a plate and keep warm whilst you whisk together the dressing ingredients and assemble the salad ingredients on individual plates. Slice the still-warm duck breasts into thin diagonal slivers. Arrange these on top of each assembled salad. Pour a little dressing over each salad. A few butter-fried bread croutons can be added for extra crunch if liked. These, too, should be warm.

Warm duck salad

GADO GADO

The supreme salad of South East Asia; it's often eaten
as a snack but it can form a full, light meal.

INGREDIENTS

Serves 4

1 crisp lettuce (or 12 blanched cabbage leaves)
225 g/8 oz new potatoes, scrubbed
225 g/8 oz green beans, topped and tailed
½ cucumber, washed and halved lengthways
4 hard-boiled eggs
225 g/8 oz small tomatoes, skinned and halved
225 g/8 oz beansprouts

FOR THE SAUCE:

4 tbsp crunchy peanut butter
1 tbsp soy sauce
2 tsp fresh lemon juice
2 tsp soft brown sugar
125 ml/4 fl oz water

Lay the lettuce or cabbage leaves on a large oval serving-plate.
Boil the potatoes until they're just tender, then put into cold water to cool.
Cook the green beans for 7 minutes until they're done but still
crunchy and allow them to cool.

Scoop out the seeds of the cucumber and cut into wafer-thin half moons.
Shell the eggs and cut into quarters or eighths. Cut the potatoes in half.
Arrange rings of cucumber slices, tomatoes, egg, potatoes and beans
on top of the lettuce or cabbage. Sprinkle the beansprouts
and remaining cucumber slices over the top.

To make the sauce, put all the ingredients into a non-stick pan, bring to the boil,
stirring, and allow to simmer gently for 5 minutes. The final sauce should
have the consistency of single cream; if it needs a little more water,
add it when it has boiled. Allow the sauce to cool and pour
a little over the salad. Serve the rest separately.

Gado gado

WALDORF SALAD

This is said to have been invented at the Waldorf Astoria Hotel in New York
at the beginning of this century. It could be true as Americans
have a gift for 'meal' salads that's second to none.

INGREDIENTS   Serves 4

2 crisp apples (contrasting colours)
1 head celery
115 g/4 oz walnut halves
225 g/8 oz cooked chicken breast, skinned and boned
Juice of ½ lemon
Salt and freshly ground black pepper
150 ml/5 fl oz mayonnaise (home-made or a good quality bought one)
Lettuce cups from Little Gem or Iceberg lettuce
Celery leaves, to garnish

Core, but don't peel the apples and cut them into 1 cm/½ in chunks. Wash the
inner stalks of the celery and cut them into similar-sized pieces. Roughly chop most
of the walnut halves, saving a few for decoration.

Slice the chicken breast then mix the apples, celery, chopped walnuts and chicken
with the lemon juice. Season the mixture and add the mayonnaise. Stir well and
chill for 30 minutes. Serve the salad in lettuce cups garnished with walnut halves
and celery leaves.

ROCKET, PRAWN
AND TOMATO SALAD

Rocket is a salad leaf that was very familiar in Britain in the seventeenth century;
it later dropped out of use but recently became fashionable again. It's now readily
available and used as it is in this first-course salad, it adds colour and bite to the
mixture. The tomatoes to use are the smallest cherry tomatoes you can find, often
sold under names like Gardener's Delight or Flavia, but the thing to look for is
small tomatoes with a bright, full colour.

INGREDIENTS

115 g/4 oz rocket
225 g/8 oz cherry tomatoes
175 g/6 oz peeled prawns

FOR THE DRESSING: Serves 2

3 tbsp salad oil, preferably olive
1 tbsp red wine vinegar
Pinch of salt
Pinch of sugar
1 tsp Dijon mustard

Wash and dry the rocket leaves and tear them in half. Remove the stalks of the
tomatoes and cut them in half. Put the dressing ingredients into a jar or bowl and
shake or whisk until smoothly blended.

Mix the rocket, tomatoes and prawns together and pile into two cups or serving-
dishes. Pour some of the dressing over each one and refrigerate for approximately
half an hour for the flavours to develop before serving.

Waldorf salad (top) with Rocket, prawn and tomato salad

ORANGE AND ALMOND DATE SALAD

This is a lovely fragrant fruit salad with which to end a meal. It combines the oranges for which Morocco is now famous with dates and almonds traditionally grown there for centuries. The recipe calls for a little orange-flower water, which is available in the home baking section of your supermarket or from a chemist.

INGREDIENTS
6 large oranges
10 fresh dates (dried ones will do
  but aren't as nice)
55 g/2 oz almonds, cut into
  slivers and toasted
1 tsp orange-flower water
½ tsp ground cinnamon

Serves 4

Peel the oranges, making sure you get rid of all the white bits, and slice them thinly across to make about 6–7 slices per orange. Arrange these prettily around a shallow bowl. Stone and finely chop the dates and sprinkle them in a ring around the outside of the oranges. Sprinkle the slivered almonds in an inner ring. Spoon any juice out of the dish and mix it with the orange-flower water then pour it back over the oranges, dates and almonds. This will keep in the fridge for a couple of hours and indeed it's best served chilled. Just before you serve it, sprinkle the whole confection with a little ground cinnamon.

HOT BAKED FRUIT SALAD

We tend to think of fruit salad as consisting only of fresh fruit, but in fact the idea of a cooked fruit salad or compote goes far back in culinary history.
This hot fruit salad provides an unusual way of using simple, everyday ingredients.
The spices bring out the flavours of the fruit in a most enticing way.

INGREDIENTS
2 apples
2 pears
1 large orange
2 satsumas or tangerines
2 bananas
2 tbsp soft brown sugar
½ tsp ground ginger
½ tsp ground cinnamon
Pinch of ground cloves
25 g/1 oz butter

Serves 4

Pre-heat the oven to 350°F/180°C/160°C Fan/Gas Mark 4.

Core the apples and pears, but don't peel them. Cut each one into 12 slices. Peel the orange and satsumas and divide them into segments. Remove any pips and pith. Peel the bananas and slice them across into 2.5 cm/1 in pieces.

Mix all the fruit together in a bowl, adding the sugar and spices, and stir so it's thoroughly coated. Spoon the fruit into a baking-dish and dot with butter. Bake for 25 minutes. Take it out, spoon the juices over the fruit and bake for another 20 minutes. The fruit should just start to caramelise by the end of this time. I like this hot, with a little pouring cream. On the other hand, low-fat fromage frais is better for you! You could also allow it to cool, then chill it before serving.

Orange and almond date salad

AUTUMN FRUIT SALAD WITH THYME AND GINGER

This is a simple autumn compote flavoured with thyme and ginger, unexpected as a combination for fruit but marvellously effective nonetheless. You can chill this compote but perhaps best of all, eat it while it's still warm.

INGREDIENTS   Serves 4

150 ml/5 fl oz water
55 g/2 oz caster sugar
25 g/1 oz stem ginger in syrup
1 large orange
2 eating apples
2 slightly under-ripe pears
115 g/4 oz green grapes, preferably seedless
1 large sprig fresh or 1 tsp dried thyme

Heat the water, sugar and a couple of tablespoons of syrup from the stem ginger jar together in a pan and bring to the boil to make a clear syrup.

Peel the orange and slice it across the grain into rounds 5 mm/¼ in thick – remove any pips. Cut each apple in half, remove the cores and quarter. Cut the pears in half lengthways, remove the cores and cut into quarters. Remove the grapes from their stalks and, if they have seeds, halve and de-pip them.

Put the apples and pears into the syrup and simmer for 5 minutes. Add the thyme (if it's dried put it in a muslin bag so that you can retrieve it without it coating the fruit). Add the orange slices and continue to simmer for another 5 minutes.

Slice the pieces of stem ginger as thinly as you can, add these to the pan along with the grapes and simmer for 5 minutes more. Pour into a shallow gratin dish or similar china or glass container, remove the thyme and allow the mixture to cool a little before eating.

Autumn fruit salad with thyme and ginger (top) and Hot baked fruit salad (see page 60)

Numbers in italic type refer to illustrations